Does Your Flamingo Flamenco?

The Best Little Dictionary of Confusing Words and Malapropisms

More books by Arlene Miller, The Grammar Diva

- *The Best Little Grammar Book Ever: 101 Ways to Impress With Your Writing and Speaking (First Edition)*—paperback and e-book

- *Correct Me If I'm Wrong: Getting Your Grammar, Punctuation, and Word Usage Right*—paperback and e-book

- *The Great Grammar Cheat Sheet: 50 Grammar, Punctuation, Writing, and Word Usage Tips You Can Use Now*—e-book

- *Beyond Worksheets: Creative Lessons for Teaching Grammar in Middle School and High School*—e-book

- *The Best Grammar Workbook Ever: Grammar, Punctuation, and Word Usage for Ages 10 Through 110*—paperback and e-book

- *Fifty Shades of Grammar: Scintillating and Saucy Sentences, Syntax, and Semantics from The Grammar Diva*—paperback and e-book

- *The Best Little Grammar Workbook Ever! Use Alone or with Its Companion Book:* The Best Little Grammar Book Ever, Second Edition—paperback and e-book

---

If you are the proud owner of any of these books, we always appreciate reviews on Amazon, Goodreads, or your favorite website.

Thank you!

Does Your Flamingo Flamenco?

The Best Little Dictionary of Confusing Words and Malapropisms

Arlene Miller THE GRAMMAR DIVA

bigwords101
Petaluma, California

Does Your Flamingo Flamenco? The Best Little Dictionary of Confusing Words and Malapropisms

Cover art and design by Matt Hinrichs
Interior design and formatting by Marny K. Parkin

Publisher's Cataloging-in-Publication Data

Library of Congress Control Number: 2017900175

Miller, Arlene. Does Your Flamingo Flamenco? The Best Little Dictionary of Confusing Words and Malapropisms, 2017

p. cm.

ISBN 978-0-9911674-8-7

1. English language—Grammar. 2. English language—Usage. 3. English language—Terms and Phrases.

Library of Congress: PE 1460.F576 2017
Dewey: 428.1

Published by bigwords101, P.O. Box 4483, Petaluma, CA 94955 USA

website and blog: www.bigwords101.com

Contact Ingram, Baker & Taylor, or the publisher for quantity discounts for your company, organization, or educational institution.

To Jake and Shelley,
As Always

Contents

Part 2: Malapropisms   57

Contact and Ordering Information   **67**

Acknowledgements

This is my ninth grammar book, so thank you to everyone who has kept me on the path! I never thought I would write two grammar books, let alone nine (and still counting).

Special thanks to Marny Parkin, my interior book designer, and Matt Hinrichs, my cover designer. These two talented people have been with me for nearly the entire journey.

More special thanks goes to Gil Namur, who has designed and kept my website beautiful! And I cannot forget my local independent bookstore, Copperfield's Books, for allowing me to launch each book there, as well as give talks and workshops—and for stocking my books on their shelves.

Thank you to the members of BAIPA (Bay Area Independent Publishers Association) and Redwood Writers (a branch of California Writers Club) for your generosity, support, and knowledge.

Thank you to my friends and family.

Arlene Miller
The Grammar Diva

Introduction

Does Your Flamingo Flamenco? The Best Little Dictionary of Confusing Words and Malapropisms is a compilation, in alphabetical order, of commonly confused words. Some of these words include *affect* and *effect; lay* and *lie; assure, ensure,* and *insure; compliment* and *complement.* You get the picture.

The second part of the book lists common malapropisms, words and phrases used incorrectly—and sometimes unintentionally humorously. Although there is some overlap of malapropisms and confusing words, most of the malapropisms are phrases and idioms. They are also listed alphabetically.

The complete table of contents and alphabetical presentation make an index unnecessary.

If you have any comments about this book, or if you have a question about something that is not included here (and you think it should be), please contact me. I can be reached at info@bigwords101.com. You may be interested in visiting my website at www.bigwords101.com and signing up for my weekly blog.

Conventions Used in This Book

1. I have used italics in examples and to indicate words used as themselves.

2. I have used a conversational tone in this book to make it easy to read.

Arlene Miller, The Grammar Diva

Part 1
Confusing Words

A

Accede/Exceed

Accede: To give in or agree to—I will *accede* to this plan.

Exceed: To go beyond the limit; surpass—The results *exceeded* my expectations.

Accept/Except

Accept: To take what is offered—I will *accept* your thoughtful gift.

Except: Leaving out; other than—Everyone is going *except* me.

Access/Assess

Access: The ability to approach—There is no *access* to the roof from here.

Assess: Estimate or judge the value or character of—I *assessed* the damages to the house.

Accidentally/Accidently

Accidentally: Happening by accident—I *accidentally* dropped the plate and broke it.

Accidently: Not a word.

Adapt/Adept/Adopt

Adapt: To adjust or make suitable—The puppy *adapted* well to its new family.

Adept: Highly skilled or expert—She is quite *adept* at welding.

Adopt: To take into one's family; to accept and use an idea—We *adopted* the new puppy last week.

After we *adapted* the tool so that left-handed people could use it, she became quite *adept* at quilting, and she *adopted* the style we use in our business.

Addition/Edition

Addition: Joining one thing to another—The soup was better with the *addition* of salt.

Edition: A specific version of a book, newspaper, newsletter, etc.—I just bought the fourth *edition* of that dictionary.

Adverse/Averse

Adverse: Unfavorable (seldom used with people)—These are *adverse* weather conditions for hiking!

Averse: Feeling against something (used with people)—She was *averse* to all our plans.

Advice/Advise

These two words are different parts of speech and are pronounced differently.

Advice: The *c* has an *s* sound, and the word is a noun—I have some good *advice* for you.

Advise: The *s* has a *z* sound, and the word is a verb—Could you *advise* me on this legal matter?

Affect/Effect

Affect: Usually a verb, an action—The sunshine *affects* my mood positively.

Effect: Usually a noun, a thing—The rain has a negative *effect* on my mood.

Affect: Occasionally a noun (pronounced with the stress on the first syllable and a short *a,* meaning "a way of acting")—The girl has a strange *affect.*

Effect: Occasionally a verb, meaning "to cause"—The new leader will *effect* some changes in the policies.

Age/Aged

Age: This word is used as a noun or present tense verb—He is the same *age* as I am. He never seems to *age* at all.

Aged: This word is used as an adjective (describing word) or past tense of the verb—These apartments are for the *aged* population. This boy, *aged* 10, is my student. His mother has *aged* in the past year.

Allusion/Illusion/Elude

Allusion: A reference to something (its verb is *to allude)*—She made an *allusion* to Shakespeare in her speech about famous playwrights.

Illusion: Something you see that isn't there—The water you sometimes think you see ahead on the highway is just an *illusion.* (There is no *illude.*)

Elude: To escape detection—He ran behind the building, *eluding* the police.

Almost/Most

The general rule: If you can use *almost* in a sentence, use it.

Almost: *Almost* everyone is here by now. (Since *almost* fits here, don't say *most everyone.*)

Most: *Most* of the pizza is gone. (*Almost* doesn't make sense here, so use *most.*)

Alot/A lot/Allot

Alot: Not a word. Don't use it.

A lot: Many or frequently. Use a better word if you can find one.— I have *a lot* of friends. (*I have many friends* is better.)

Allot: To distribute or assign—We children were each *allotted* five pieces of candy.

Aloud/Allowed

Aloud: Out loud—She read the poem *aloud* to the class.

Allowed: Permitted—I am *allowed* to stay out until midnight.

Already/All ready

Already: Tells when—Are you finished packing *already*?

All ready: Completely prepared—We are *all ready* to go.

Alright/All right

Alright: Isn't a word (or is a really slang word, so avoid it).

All right: Okay—If it is *all right*, I will go with you. Everything will be *all right.*

Altar/Alter

Altar: The one in a church—The couple stood at the *altar.*

Alter: To change in some way—I *altered* the speech by shortening it.

Altogether/All together

Altogether: Totally or completely—This soup is *altogether* too spicy.

All together: Everyone at once—Let's sing *all together.* Let's *all* sing *together.*

Always/All ways

Always: All the time—I *always* do my chores.

All ways: Every way—These are *all ways* to do the same math problem.

Among/Between

Among: Used with more than two people—Divide the pizza *among* the four of you.

Between: Used with two people—Divide the pizza *between* the two of you.

Amoral/Immoral

Amoral: Neither moral nor immoral; having no moral code—The *amoral* murderer doesn't know right from wrong.

Immoral: Not moral—Most people consider stealing *immoral.*

Amount/Number

Amount: Use with singulars and nouns that cannot be counted—The *amount* of sugar in that candy bar makes it full of calories.

Number: Use with plurals—The *number* of calories in that candy is enough for an entire day! (Not the *amount of calories.*)

Anecdote/Antidote

Anecdote: A little story, often humorous—He began his speech with an *anecdote* about his childhood.

Antidote: Something that remedies or counteracts disease or injury—Penicillin is an *antidote* for bacterial infections.

Annual/Annul

Annual: Happens every year—I have read the *annual* report for the company.

Annul: To abolish or cancel (often used with marriages)—The new rules were fortunately *annulled*, since they made no sense.

Anxious/Eager

Anxious: Worried or distressed—I am *anxious* about the big math test.

Eager: Looking forward to; earnest—He is *eager* to begin his vacation.

Anymore/Any more

Anymore: Any longer (usually used with a negative)—I don't eat meat *anymore*.

Any more: Additional—I don't want *any more* pasta.

Anyone/Any one

Anyone: Refers to a person—Is *anyone* there?

Any one: Doesn't necessarily refer to a person, and is generally followed by *of*—*Any one* of these tickets could be the winning one.

Anytime/Any time

Anytime: Whenever; at any time—Come over and visit me *anytime*.

Any time: Some amount of time—Do you have *any time* to fix the door?

Anyway/Anyways/Any way

Anyways: Not a word. That goes for *anywheres, everywheres,* and *somewheres.*

Anyway: Anyhow—You can have it; I never liked pizza *anyway*.

Any way: In any manner—You can get there *any way* you want.

Appraise/Apprise

Appraise: To estimate the value of—She *appraised* the ring at $2,000.

Apprise: To inform—We were not *apprised* about the meeting this morning.

As if/Like

As if: Used before a group of words with a subject and verb—She acted *as if* she were a queen.

Like: Used in a simple comparison, usually before a noun—She acted *like* a queen.

Ascent/Assent

Ascent: The act of climbing or going up—The *ascent* was steep and dangerous.

Assent: To agree (verb); agreement (noun)—He *assented* to the plan by nodding.

Assistance/Assistants

Assistance: Help—Do you need *assistance* getting up the stairs?

Assistants: Plural of *assistant*; helper—The teacher has two *assistants*.

Assure/Ensure/Insure

Assure: To promise—I *assure* you that it will all turn out fine.

Ensure: To make sure—I will *ensure* that the house is safe for you to live in.

Insure: To protect the value of (usually money related)—I *insured* the ring for $5,000.

Awhile/A while

Awhile: For a while (can be replaced by those three words)—Please stay *awhile*.

A while: Cannot be replaced with "for a while"—It has been *a while* since I have seen her.

B

Bad/Badly

Bad: Adjective. Used to describe a noun or used after a verb of being or sense (for example, *is, smells, feels, tastes, sounds*)—The dog is *bad*. The *bad* dog barked. The dog smells *bad*.

Badly: Adverb. Describes a verb—She cooks *badly*. I play tennis *badly*.

Baited/Bated

Baited: Prepared a fishing rod with bait—I *baited* the hook.

Bated: Usually used in the phrase, "I waited with *bated* breath."

Bazaar/Bizarre

Bazaar: Marketplace—We visited a large outdoor *bazaar* in China.

Bizarre: Weird—She talked about seeing aliens and other *bizarre* events.

Because of/Due to

Because of: Means "as a result of" and is **not** used after the verb *to be* (*is*, for example)—She is afraid of dogs *because of* being bitten several times. (*Not* Her fear of dogs is because of being bitten as a child.)

Due to: Means "the result of" or "resulting from" and is always used after a form of *to be*. Her fear of dogs *was due to* being attacked when she was child.

Berth/Birth

Berth: A place, often for sleeping—I had a small *berth* on the train.

Birth: Coming into being—We celebrated the *birth* of her new baby.

Beside/Besides

Beside: Next to—I sat *beside* him on the airplane.

Besides: In addition; furthermore; otherwise—There is no one here *besides* me.

Between: See *Among.*

Biannual/Biennial

Biannual: Twice a year—The *biannual* catalog comes out every January and June.

Biennial: Every two years—Every other year we have a *biennial* talent show.

Bimonthly/Semimonthly

Bimonthly: Generally every two months—This magazine is *bimonthly*, with six editions a year.

Semimonthly: Generally, twice a month—This *semimonthly* journal is published the first and third weeks of each month.

Blond/Blonde

Blond: A person with light hair—All her children are *blond*.

Blonde: a female with light hair—She has always been a *blonde*.

Board/Bored

Board: Flat piece of wood—I sawed the *board* in half.

Bored: Not interested—I was really *bored* watching that dull movie.

Born/Borne

Born: Brought forth by birth—He was *born* on July 4th.

Borne: Past participle of the verb *to bear*—She has *borne* six children.

Both/Each

Both: One and the other together—We are *both* going on vacation.

Each: Each one individually—*Each* of you should take a cookie.

Brake/Break

Brake: To stop; something that stops something—Step on the *brakes*!

Break: To smash or hurt; a gap—Don't *break* the vase. There is a *break* in the traffic.

Bring/Take (These words go in opposite directions.)

Bring: You bring something back—*Bring* me some coffee from the kitchen.

Take: You take something away—*Take* these dishes to the kitchen.

Buy/By/Bye

Buy: To purchase something—I want to *buy* a new car.

By: A preposition—This book is written *by* my friend. Stand *by* the window.

Bye: Farewell; the preferential status of an athlete—The gymnast received a *bye* into the semifinals. "*Bye* for now," she said.

By accident/On accident

By accident: Accidentally—I dropped the eggs *by accident*.

On accident: Don't use it. *By accident* is always the correct way to say it.

C

Canvas/Canvass

Canvas: Fabric used in shoes, backpacks, tents, etc.—Can I put my *canvas* shoes in the washer?

Canvass: To solicit orders, votes, subscriptions, etc.—She *canvassed* the neighborhood, taking a poll.

Capital/Capitol

Capital: Pertaining to the city that is capital of a state, capital letters, and money—Boston is the *capital* of Massachusetts. Make that a capital *A*.

Capitol: Refers only to the actual building—When we were in Boston, we visited the state *Capitol.*

Censor/Censure

Censor: To ban or prohibit something—Many books have been *censored* over the years, including some classics that are now read in schools.

Censure: Strong disapproval; an official reprimand—A group of senators *censured* the President on his policies with foreign countries.

Censor/Sensor

Censor: To ban or prohibit something—That movie has been *censored* and will not be shown to the public.

Sensor: A device sensitive to light, sounds, etc., that transmits a measurement—The *sensor* can tell if there is the smallest amount of movement in the room.

Cite/Site/Sight

Cite: To quote, mention, or refer to something—She *cited* my new book in her speech.

Site: Refers to a place—There was an accident at the construction *site.*

Sight: Something you see—That fallen tree was quite a *sight*!

Climactic/Climatic

Climactic: Comes from *climax*—The dull movie's ending was anti-*climactic*.

Climatic: Relating to the weather—Global warming has produced many *climatic* changes.

Close/Clothes

Close: Opposite of *open*; opposite of *far*—Please *close* the door when you leave. I live *close* by.

Clothes: Things you wear—I am buying some new *clothes* for the trip.

Clothes/Cloths

Clothes: Things you wear—I need some new *clothes*.

Cloths: (Pronounced with a short *o*.) Pieces of fabric, rags—I ran out of dry *cloths* while washing my car.

Coarse/Course

Coarse: Lacking in fineness; made of large parts; vulgar—The sand on this beach is *coarse*, made up of large grains, instead of fine, as we prefer it.

Course: A direction or route to be taken—I am taking this *course* of action to get rid of my cold.

Collaborate/Corroborate

Collaborate: To work together on something—We three students are *collaborating* on the science project.

Corroborate: To confirm or make more certain—She *corroborated* her friend's story that they were at the library and not at the mall.

Come/Go (These words go in opposite directions.)

Come: Approach; travel toward—My brother is *coming* home soon.

Go: To leave or go away from—I am *going* to Spain next month.

Common/Mutual

Common: Shared—My sister and I have several friends in *common*.

Mutual: Reciprocal—We have *mutual* admiration for each other, I for her intelligence and she for my wit.

Complement/Compliment

Complement: To go together well—The dress *complements* your green eyes.

Compliment: To say something nice—The man *complimented* his date on her beauty. (*Complimentary* means *free*.)

Compose/Comprise

Compose: To make up—Fifty states *compose* the United States. (The parts compose the whole.) The United States *is composed of* fifty states.

Comprise: To be made up of—The United States *comprises* fifty states. (The whole comprises the parts.)

Do not use "is comprised of."

Conscience/Conscious

Conscience: The thing that gets guilty and tells you that you may have done something wrong—My *conscience* told me I was doing something unwise.

Conscious: Aware of what is going on—After the accident I was relieved to see that he was *conscious*.

Consecutive/Successive

Following in order or an uninterrupted sequence. These words are interchangeable.

There are three *consecutive* meetings on Friday morning, at 9, 10, and 11 a.m.

There are three *successive* meetings on Friday morning, at 9, 10, and 11 a.m.

Contingency/Contingent

Contingency: Something dependent on the fulfillment of a condition—One *contingency* in the deal is that we sell our house by July 31.

Contingent: An assembled group—The *contingent* included all graduating students.

Continual/Continuous: (These words have slightly different meanings.)

Continual: Happening over and over again, often in rapid succession—The *continual* snowstorms this winter have made clearing all the snow very difficult.

Continuous: Without stopping—We have had *continuous* rain all day without a break.

Copyright/Copy write

Copyright: Legal term for protecting work—I *copyrighted* my book last year.

Copy write: To write copy, as a copywriter—My job is to *copy write* for cell phone advertisements.

Could of/Would of/Should of

You're right! These are wrong! It is *could have, would have,* and *should have!* (You can use *could've, should've,* and *would've* if you want, but I don't really like these contractions.)

I *could have* eaten that whole pizza.

I *would have* gone if you had asked me.

You *should have* told me about it.

(Obviously, *woulda, shoulda,* and *coulda* are unacceptable!)

Credible/Creditable

Credible: Believeable—The witness had a very *credible* story.

Creditable: Worthy of credit, honor—She has done a *creditable* job as union president.

Criteria/Criterion

Standard(s) of judging something

Criterion is singular—You need to meet one more *criterion* before you can be considered for the promotion.

Criteria is plural—These are the four *criteria* for getting into the advanced class.

Currant/Current

Currant: A small berry—She made some *currant* jam.

Current: New; most recent—Is this the *current* edition of the newspaper?

D

Data/Datum

Information

Datum is singular and rarely used.

Data is plural, but is usually now used with a singular verb and considered singular—The *data* is in, and it shows that crime has gone down in the past three years.

Desert/Dessert

There are three of these to confuse. There is the sweet one, the dry one, and the lonely one.

Desert: A very dry place—Camels generally are found in the *desert*.

Desert: To leave alone—If you *desert* your fellow soldiers, you will be in big trouble. (Pronounced that same as the sweet one.)

Dessert: A sweet treat—I am having the apple pie for *dessert.*

Different from/Different than

Different from: Correct in comparisons—This dress is *different from* the one you just bought.

Different than: Do not use.

Discreet/Discrete

Discreet: The one having to do with keeping a secret—Please be *discreet* with the information I just gave you.

Discrete: Separate—Please put these folders into three *discrete* piles by color.

Disinterested/Uninterested

Disinterested: Impartial, having no interest in the outcome—We need a *disinterested* person to determine which team will go first.

Uninterested: Not interested—I am *uninterested* in football.

Distinct/Distinctive

Distinct: Separate; different from—These letters show two *distinct* handwriting styles.

Distinctive: Having a certain style; notable—I recognized her by her *distinctive* voice.

Dived/Dove

These two words are both perfectly fine past tenses of the verb *dive.* Use whichever you wish, but be consistent in the same piece of writing.

He *dove* into the pool. He *dived* into the pool. You choose.

Doubt that/Doubt whether

Doubt that: Use when you don't think something is true—I *doubt that* she will show up.

Doubt whether: Use when there is uncertainty—I *doubt* whether there has been enough rain to stop the drought.

Dual/Duel

Dual: Two—This *dual*-purpose machine both grinds and brews the coffee.

Duel: Fight between two people—The cowboys decided who was boss with a *duel*.

Due to: See *Because of.*

E

e.g./i.e.

These abbreviations come from Latin. Remember to use a period after each letter, and a comma both before and after the abbreviation.

e.g.: *Exempli gratia*, or "for example"—Long-haired dogs, *e.g.,* poodles, don't shed or cause allergies.

i.e.: *Id est*, or "that is"—The shortest month of the year, *i.e.,* February, has only 28 days.

etc.

This abbreviation comes from Latin and is not to be confused with *e.g.* or *i.e.* It is usually used at the end of the sentence and is preceded by a comma.

etc: And the others—Music genres include jazz, rock, pop, classical, country, rap, *etc.*

Each other/One another

These two phrases are interchangeable. Some people say that *each other* should be used when referring to two people, and *one another* should be used when referring to more than two people, but this distinction is unnecessary and not often used—We should all be kind to *each other*. In this classroom, we are all kind to *one another*.

Each: See *Both.*

Eager: See *Anxious.*

Earth/earth

Does *earth* begin with a capital *E?* Sometimes.

Earth: The only time you begin *earth* with a capital *E* is when you are using it in the same sentence or context with other heavenly bodies that *are* capitalized. (The names of the other planets are capitalized, but *sun* and *moon* are not.)—Both Jupiter and Saturn are larger than *Earth.*

earth: Recycling is just one of the ways in which we can take care of the *earth.*

Edition: See *Addition.*

Effect: See *Affect.*

Elicit/Illicit

Elicit: To draw or bring forth—He was so shy the teacher could not *elicit* a single answer from him.

Illicit: Unlawful or immoral—The governor was put in prison because of the *illicit* acts he was accused of.

Elude: See *Allusion.*

Emigrate/Immigrate

Emigrate: The prefix *-e* means *out*, so to *emigrate* means to leave a country—They *emigrated* from Russia to the United States.

Immigrate: To go *to* a country—They left Russia and *immigrated* to the United States.

Eminent/Imminent

Eminent: Well-known or renowned in one's field—Dr. Ray is an *eminent* scientist in the field of cosmology.

Imminent: About to happen—Looking at the dark sky, I would say a storm is *imminent*.

Ensure: See *Assure.*

Every day/Everyday

Every day: Daily; each day—I exercise *every day*.

Everyday: Adjective that describes something that happens every day—Exercise is an *everyday* occurrence for me.

Every one/Everyone

Every one: Each of them; every single one—*Every one* of the children passed the test.

Everyone: Everybody—*Everyone* on the list is coming to the party.

Exceed: See *Accede.*

Exceedingly/Excessively

Exceedingly: Very; extremely—He is *exceedingly* tall.

Excessively: More than proper or necessary—The students were chatting *excessively* during my lecture.

Except: See *Accept.*

F

Fair/Fare

Fair: (multiple meanings) Just; a carnival; just okay—They sell cotton candy at the *fair.* I thought the judging was *fair.* The food isn't very good; it's *fair.*

Fare: (multiple meanings) Cost of something; something offered to the public as entertainment—The bus *fare* is 50 cents. The wedding offered delicious *fare* for dinner.

Farther/Further

Farther: Has to do with distance—I live *farther* away from work than you do.

Further: Any more or longer—I cannot discuss this any *further.*

Fewer/Less

Fewer: Use with plurals and things that can be counted—There are *fewer cookies* on this plate than on the other one.

Less: Use with singulars or things that cannot be counted—There is *less sugar* in these cookies.

Figuratively/Literally

Figuratively: Involving a figure of speech, likely a metaphor; so called—Working in a small company, she was a big fish in a small pond, *figuratively* speaking.

Literally: Actually; really—I was telling a joke, but unfortunately she took it *literally* and was insulted.

Firstly, Secondly, Thirdly, Lastly

These are **transition words**. Use *first, second, third,* and *last* instead of adding *-ly* at the end (and please don't use *first off*)—*First,* add sugar. *Second,* add butter. *Third,* blend them together. *Last,* add the flour.

Flair/Flare

Flair: Style or natural talent—She has a *flair* for home design.

Flare: To burn or suddenly burst forth—Her temper *flared* when he insulted her.

Flamenco/Flamingo

Flamenco: A type of dance—I missed my *flamenco* lesson last week.

Flamingo: Pink bird that often stands on one leg—I saw *flamingoes* at the zoo.

Flammable/Inflammable/Nonflammable (Confusion alert!)

Flammable: Easily set on fire—Be careful with that fabric near the flame as it is very *flammable.*

Inflammable: Same as *flammable*; easily set on fire—I never buy *inflammable* blankets because they don't protect the baby from fire.

Nonflammable: Not flammable—I always buy *nonflammable* fabrics because they are safer in case of fire.

Foreword/Forward

Foreword: A brief introduction in a book, often written by someone other than the author—The *foreword* of this book was written by a famous poet.

Forward: Toward; in the direction of—Please step *forward* when I call your name.

(Please note the difference in spelling: one is *ward* and the other is *word*.)

Formally/Formerly

Formally: Involves tuxedos and gowns and is from the word *formal*—You need to dress *formally* for the wedding.

Formerly: What happened before; from the word *former*—Jane Smith was *formerly* known as Jane Mills until she got married.

Former/Latter

Former: If you mentioned two things, the first one you mentioned.

Latter: If you mentioned two things, the *latter* is the second one you mentioned.

I have two dogs, a Chihuahua and a great Dane. The *former* is named Tiny, and the *latter i*s named Big Boy.

Forth/Fourth

Forth: Forward—The trees swayed back and *forth*.

Fourth: The one after *third*. He is in *fourth* grade.

Found/Founded

Found: The past tense of find—I *found* a rock in my shoe.

Founded: The past tense of *found* when it means "to establish"—He *founded* the charity last year.

Further: See *Farther.*

G

Gibe/Jibe/Jive

Gibe: To taunt; a taunt or sarcastic remark—The bully would *gibe* the poor girl every day. (Can also be spelled *jibe.*)

Jibe: To agree with or be in harmony with—Her explanation *jibes* with his story.

Jive: Swing or early jazz music; the jargon of such music—*Jive* was popular when my mom was a kid, and she still likes it.

Go: See *Come*.

Good/Well

Good is an adjective, generally used to describe a noun. *Well* is an adverb, usually used to describe an action verb. Adjectives, however, are used after *sense* or *being* verbs (for example, the verbs *to be, to look, to taste, to feel,* etc.) Note that even though it is an adverb, *well* can be used after sense or being verbs to indicate a state of health (as in the last example below).

He plays tennis *well.*

I did *well* on the test.

Spot is a *good* dog.

That cake *looks good.* (Adjective after "sense" verb.)

I feel *good.* (Adjective after "sense" verb.)

I feel *well.* (Adverb also correct: state of health.)

Gorilla/Guerilla

Gorilla: They are in the zoo—The *gorillas* are my favorite animals in the zoo.

Guerilla: A type of warfare—The terrorists used *guerilla* warfare.

Got/Have

Got: Received (as the past tense of *get*)—I *got* a new bike for my birthday.

Have: To own or possess something—I *have* a new bike. (Not *I have got a new bike.*)

H

Hanged/Hung

Hanged: The past tense of *hang* only when there is a noose involved—I heard that the man who committed suicide *hanged* himself.

Hung: The past tense of *hang* when it refers to almost anything except a person—I *hung* a picture to hide a hole in the wall.

Have: See *Got.*

Healthful/Healthy

Healthful: Something that provides you with good health—That wheatgrass and kale smoothie is very *healthful.*

Healthy: Possessing good health—I will be *healthy* if I exercise and drink that wheatgrass and kale smoothie.

Hoard/Horde

Hoard: A collection of stuff, or to collect an overabundance of stuff, sometimes secretly—She *hoards* chocolate and hides it under her bed.

Horde: A large group of people—*Hordes* of people lined the street for the parade.

Home/Hone

Home: That place where you live—It is good to be *home.*

Hone: To sharpen or improve—Over time she *honed* her cooking skills to the point where she was a better cook than her mother.

However/Therefore

These are not confusing words to use. What *is* confusing is knowing when to put commas around these words and when you need a semicolon (or a period). Look at these examples.

I think, *therefore,* that I am right and you are wrong.

I studied; *therefore,* I did well on the test.

Here is what you do: take out *however* or *therefore,* and read the sentence without it. If you have a sentence, commas are fine. However, if you are left with a run-on sentence (two sentences), you need a period or a semicolon. In the first example above, the commas are fine; the sentence without *therefore* reads, "I think that I am right and you are wrong." In the second sentence, if you take out *therefore,* you get, "I studied, I did well on the test." Since that is a run-on sentence, you need a semicolon or a period before *therefore.* Or, you can add a conjunction and keep the commas. (*I study and, therefore, I do well on my tests.*) *However* is treated exactly the same way.

I

I could care less

Yes, this one is still around. Now think about it. If you *could* care less, you care some and you probably wouldn't be talking about this at all. You are making the comment because you don't care at all. Therefore, you *couldn't care less* is the correct way to say or write it.

i.e.: See *e.g.*

Idle/Idol

Idle: Not doing anything; not in use—My exercise bike has been *idle* for months!

Idol: Someone you look up to—His many hit songs make him an *idol* with teenage girls.

If/Whether

If is often used when *whether* should be used.

If: Conditional—I will not go hiking *if* it rains.

Whether: Implies a choice—I don't know *whether* I should take the bus or walk to work. (Not *if.*)

When *or not* appears in the sentence, use *whether*—I don't know *whether* or not I should go.

Illicit: See *Elicit.*

Illusion: See *Allusion.*

Immigrate: See *Emigrate.*

Imminent: See *Eminent.*

Immoral: See *Amoral.*

Imply/Infer

These two words go in different directions. *Imply* is sending the information out, and *infer* is taking the information in.

Imply: To suggest or hint at something without coming right out and saying it—Her big smile *implied* that she was thrilled with the gift.

Infer: To assume something from information you have—I *inferred* from her big smile that she was happy with the gift.

In regard to/In regards to

They both mean *concerning.*

In regard to: Preferred—*In regard to* your question, I am not attending.

In regards to: Acceptable, but more informal. Use *in regard to.*

In to/Into

Usually, there is no problem with making this one word or two. But sometimes, it really matters:

I turned my car *into* the shopping mall. This implies that some magic was done! (Should be *in to the shopping mall* to avoid confusion.)

I turned my book *into* the library. Another magic trick!

Most of the time *into* as one word will work fine! But sometimes the "in" goes more with the verb, as in the two examples (*turn in*).

Incidentally/Incidently

Incidentally: By the way—*Incidentally*, my friend is coming along with us.

Incidently: Not a word. You mean *incidentally*.

Incite/Insight

Incite: To stir up or encourage—A few people in the crowd *incited* a riot.

Insight: Intuitive knowledge—He showed great *insight* into what the poet meant.

Indexes/Indices

They are both the plural of *index*: Added information at the end of a book, or some type of marker—That history book has ten *indexes*. Financial *indices* show a rise in tech stocks. Note that *indexes,* not *indices,* is usually used for the part of a book.

Inflammable: See *Flammable.*

Insure: See *Assure.*

Intolerable/Intolerant

Intolerable: Unbearable—When I fractured my arm, I suffered *intolerable* pain.

Intolerant: Not accepting views or people different than oneself—Many wars are caused by *intolerance* of other beliefs.

Irregardless

This "word" is still around. It is a nonstandard word, so why use it? It contains two negatives: *ir-* and *-less*. The correct word is simply *regardless*. It is often followed by *of* and means *without regard to* or *in spite of*—We are going *regardless* of the weather.

Is when/Is where

These phrases should not be used. Rewrite!

No: My favorite part *is when* the dog escapes.

Yes: My favorite part is the dog's escape.

No: The best vacation *is where* you sit on the beach.

Yes: Sitting on the beach is my idea of the best vacation.

Its/It's

Its: This one is a possessive pronoun. Just like all the other possessive pronouns, it has no apostrophe: *ours, yours, his, hers, theirs*—The dog ate all *its* food.

It's: The contraction meaning "it is." ALL contractions have apostrophes: *can't, don't, couldn't, he'll,* and all the others—*It's* a beautiful day.

J

Jibe: See *Gibe.*

Jive: See *Gibe.*

K

Kind of/Sort of

These two phrases mean the same thing and are often used in an informal way that make them unnecessary in the sentence.

Kind of: It is *kind of* windy today. (No.) Kiwi is a *kind of* fruit. (Yes.) That is *kind of* you. (Yes.)

Sort of: You *sort of* turn right over there. (No.) This *sort of* behavior is unacceptable. (Yes.)

Avoid using *kind of* and *sort of* to mean "a little" or "rather."

Knew/New

Knew: Past tense of *know*—I *knew* him when he was just a baby.

New: Opposite of *old*—These are my *new* shoes.

L

Last/Latest

Last: The final one—This is the *last* album they ever put out.

Latest: The most recent one—Their *latest* song is a big hit.

Lastly: See *Firstly.*

Later/Latter

Later: At some time in the future, possibly after something else in the future—I will see you *later.* The baseball game begins *later* than the tennis match.

Latter: The last item you just mentioned—I have two cats, three fish, and a dog. I have owned the *latter* for the longest time. (That would mean the dog.)

Latter: See *Former.*

Lay/Lie:

Lay: If you are going to use *lay*, you need an object. In other words, you need to *lay* something—I am *laying* my purse on the sofa (present tense). I *laid* my purse on the sofa (past tense). I *have laid* my purse on the sofa (past participle).

Lie: Has no object—I *lie* down for my nap (present tense). Last night I *lay* on the sofa until I fell asleep (past tense). I *have lain* on that hammock every day this summer (past participle).

Note that animals and objects can *lie*, as well as people—The rocks are *lying* on the road.

Lead/Led

Lead: Present tense of this verb—They *lead* the parade every year.

Led: Past tense of the verb—He *led* the band last year.

Don't confuse these words with *read* and *read*, where the past tense is spelled the same, but pronounced differently. The past tense is pronounced *red*, but spelled *read*. The only word spelled *lead* and pronounced *led* is in your pencil.

Leave/Let

Leave: To go away from someone or something: *Leave* me alone. (Not *let* me alone.)

Let: To allow—Don't *let* the dog come into the kitchen.

Lend/Loan

Lend: A verb, or action—I will *lend* you some money.

Loan: A noun, or thing—I can give you a *loan.*

Less: See *Fewer.*

Lessen/Lesson

Lessen: To make less—The ice should *lessen* the pain from your sprain.

Lesson: The thing you have at school—I learned a *lesson* about friendship today.

Liable/Libel

Liable: Legally responsible; likely—If you break the window, you are *liable* for it. You are *liable* to break that window if you throw a ball at it.

Libel: Writing about someone to damage his or her reputation—I am suing the newspaper for *libel* because that malicious story about me is not true.

Libel/Slander

Libel: Writing about someone to damage his or her reputation—I am suing the newspaper for *libel* because that malicious story is not true.

Slander: The same as *libel* except it is spoken and not written—The governor's speech *slandered* the senator.

Licence/License

These two are the same word with different spellings. Apparently some dictionaries include *licence* with two *c*'s, but the correct spelling is with the *s*. Hard to remember? The *c* comes before the *s* in the word, just like in the alphabet.

Lightening/Lightning

Lightening: Making lighter in color or weight—She has been *lightening* her hair for years.

Lightning: Comes before the thunder in a storm—I was once nearly struck by *lightning.*

Like: See *As if.*

Literally: See *Figuratively.*

Loath/Loathe

Loath: Unwilling (adjective)—I am *loath* to fire my new employee.

Loathe: To intensely dislike (verb)—I *loathe* broccoli.

Loose/Lose

Loose: Opposite of *tight*—My pants are too *loose* because I have lost weight.

Lose: To misplace something or drop pounds—If you *lose* too much weight, your pants will be too loose.

M

Mantel/Mantle

Mantel: Frame around the opening of a fireplace—We hung the Christmas stockings on the *mantel.*

Mantle: A loose cloak or cape; something that covers or envelopes—She appeared under the *mantle* of night.

Many/Much

Many: Used for things that can be counted and plurals—I have *many* toys.

Much: Used for singulars and things that cannot be counted. There is too *much* salt in the chili.

May be/Maybe

May be: Same as *might be*—My sister *may be* coming to visit.

Maybe: Possibly—*Maybe* you can have ice cream if you finish your dinner.

May/Might

May: Implies permission or probability—Yes, you *may* go to the dance. I *may* go to the dance too.

Might: Implies possibility—I *might* go to the play, but I will probably stay home. If you had taken the other route, you *might* have had an accident in the snow!

May and *might* meaning *probability/possibility* are very close and often interchangeable. However, it is accepted that *may* is used when something is more likely to happen than when *might* is used.

Meat/Meet/Mete

Meat: You eat it if you aren't a vegetarian—I like my *meat* cooked rare.

Meet: To come together—*Meet* me in front of the mall.

Mete: To distribute or dole (out)—The cafeteria workers *meted* out the casserole to the students.

Moot/Mute

Moot: Not worth discussing—That is a *moot* point.

Mute: Silent; unable to speak—He remained *mute* throughout the trial.

More important/More importantly

More important: An adjective used most often in a comparison—It is *more important* to do your best than to win.

More importantly: An adverb used most often as a transition—I need to finish reading this book. *More importantly,* I need to get started on my project.

Most: See *Almost.*

Mutual: See *Common.*

N

New: See *Knew.*

News/Mathematics/Physics, and Other Such Singulars

Although these words end in -*s*, they are all singular and use singular verbs—The *news is* good (not *are good*). *Physics is* a difficult subject for me.

Nonflammable: See *Flammable.*

Number: See *Amount.*

O

On Accident: See *By accident.*

On/Onto

On: To be suspended from or supported by—Put your book *on* the table.

Onto: To a place or position—Climb *onto* the horse.

One another: See *Each other.*

Only

So much depends upon where you put *only* in a sentence. *Only* is generally thought to go with the word it is closest to:

Only she punched her friend in the arm. (No one else did.)

She *only punched* her friend in the arm. (She didn't do anything else.)

She punched *only her friend* in the arm. (She punched no one else.)

She punched *her only friend* in the arm. (No wonder she has no other friends!)

She punched her friend *only in the arm.* (Nowhere else.)

She punched her friend in her *only arm.* (Too bad.)

Usually, we don't make mistakes in sentences like those, but here is a common mistake in the position of *only*:

We *only have* five dollars for the movie. (Incorrect, but understandable.)

We have *only five dollars* for the movie. (Correct.)

Overdo/Overdue

Overdo: To do too much—If you *overdo* your exercise, your muscles will be sore.

Overdue: Past due—I am *overdue* for a vacation.

P

Passed/Past

Passed: Past tense of the verb *to pass*—We *passed* the school on our way home.

Past: A preposition that appears in a phrase: *past* (a/an/the) noun—We walked *past* the school on our way home.

Patience/Patients

Patience: The virtue of being able to wait without being upset—It took great *patience* to wait for the verdict in the murder trial.

Patients: The plural of *patient*, people who see the doctor—I think the doctor has too many *patients*!

Peace/Piece

Peace: The opposite of war; calmness—I wish for world *peace.*

Piece: A section of something—Would you like a *piece* of pie?

Peak/Peek/Pique

Peak: The top—We watched the sunset from the mountain *peak.*

Peek: To take a little look—I took a quick *peek* at the cake and then closed the box.

Pique: To irritate or excite—The beautiful birds *piqued* her attention.

Pedal/Peddle

Pedal: Bicycles and cars have them—Take your foot off the gas *pedal*!

Peddle: To go from place to place selling things—I have seen him *peddle* his art in my neighborhood.

Peer/Pier

Peer: A person of equal status (noun); to look out at something (verb)—I saw her *peer* at her new coworker, who was her *peer* in the department.

Pier: A structure built on posts where boats can stay—My new waterfront home even has a *pier* for my boat.

Perspective/Prospective

Perspective: The way someone sees things; viewpoint—From my *perspective,* this seems like a good idea.

Prospective: In the future; likely—My *prospective* salary will be in the six figures after my promotion.

Poor/Pore/Pour

Poor: Lacking in money or something else—I like to donate money to families *poorer* than I.

Pore: To look over very carefully—He *pored* over the contract until he was sure he understood it.

Pour: To send a liquid or other loose material from a container to something else—Be careful when you *pour* the juice into the glasses.

Pray/Prey

Pray: When you say a prayer—I go to church to *pray* for my family.

Prey: Something hunted by something else—Some people are easy *prey* for scammers.

Precede/Proceed

Precede: To come before something else—The game will *precede* the parade.

Proceed: To continue along—The parade will *proceed* down Main Street.

Premise/Premises

Premise: The reasoning upon which some idea is based—I began with the *premise* that people needed this widget I invented.

Premises: Can be the plural of *premise,* but often used to mean a building and its land—Please stay off the *premises* if you don't have business here.

Presence/Presents

Presence: The state of being somewhere—We missed your *presence* at the meeting.

Presents: Plural of *present*, or gift—I am going to open my birthday *presents* now.

Principal/Principle

Principal: (1) The head of a school—Go to the *principal's* office now! (2) The money kind—My mortgage payment consists of both *principal* and interest (3) The main one—I have a *principal* part in the dance.

Principle: Rule or ethic—My *principles* don't allow me to eat meat.

Profit/Prophet

Profit: The amount of money made—How much *profit* did your business make last year?

Prophet: An inspired teacher—People believed the old man was a *prophet* who spoke the word of God.

Prostate/Prostrate

Prostate: Gland in the male body—He had his *prostate* examined.

Prostrate: Lying flat on the ground—When I found the man, he was *prostrate* in a pool of blood.

Q

Quiet/Quite

Quiet: Not making much noise—She was as *quiet* as a mouse.

Quite: Very—The mouse was *quite* quiet.

R

Rain/Reign/Rein

Rain: Wet weather—I brought an umbrella in case it *rains.*

Reign: Period during which someone rules—The king's *reign* lasted many years.

Rein: Leather strap used by a rider to control a horse—The horse went faster as the experienced rider held on tightly to the *reins.*

Raise/Raze/Rise

Raise: To make something higher—Please *raise* the shade to let the sun in.

Raze: To tear down; demolish—We watched as they *razed* the old building.

Rise: To get up or go higher—The lake is *rising* to dangerous levels.

Note: *Raise* takes a direct object; *rise* does not. You must *raise* something.

Rapped/Rapt/Wrapped

Rapped: Past tense of *rap*; to strike quickly or to sing rap style music—I *rapped* on the door, but no one answered.

Rapt: Fully engrossed or mesmerized by something—I am a *rapt* reader of fantasy novels.

Wrapped: Past tense of *wrap*; to enclose in something folded—The newborn was snugly *wrapped* in a blanket.

Real/Really

Real: An adjective meaning *true.* It is used to describe nouns—Is that a *real* diamond?

Really: An adverb meaning *to a great extent.* It is used to describe verbs, adjectives, and other adverbs—Is she *really* baking me a cake? (Describes the verb baking.) I drive *really* slowly. (Describes the adverb *slowly*: how slowly?) The ring is *really* beautiful. (Describes the adjective *beautiful*.)

Note: Most, but not all, words ending in *-ly* are adverbs.

Reality/Realty

Reality: The state of being real—Sometimes we need to face *reality*.

Realty: Real estate—She sells *realty* on the internet.

Reason is because/Reason is that

Reason is because: Do not use this construction—The reason I am late *is because* I was stuck in traffic. (No.) I am late because I was stuck in traffic. (Yes.)

Reason is that: Use this construction—The reason I am late *is that* I was stuck in traffic.

Reference/Reverence

Reference: A mention (noun); to mention or allude to (verb)—He *referenced* the Bible many times in his speech.

Reverence: Great respect—We treated the old man with *reverence*.

Regardless: See *Irregardless.*

Regimen/Regiment

Regimen: A prescribed course that one follows—I follow a strict diet and exercise *regimen*.

Regiment: Group of ground forces in the military; to manage a group in a rigid manner—The leader of the *regimented* group was disliked because of his strictness.

Regretful/Regrettable

Regretful: Full of regret; people are usually regretful—I am *regretful* that I didn't study harder when I was younger.

Regrettable: To be regretted; circumstances are regrettable—It is *regrettable* that I didn't make better use of my education.

Residents/Residence

Residence: A place to live—I thought the building was a business, but it is a *residence*.

Residents: Plural of *resident*; someone who lives someplace—The *residents* needed to be evacuated during the hurricane.

Respectfully/Respectively

Respectfully: With respect—They listened *respectfully* when the teacher spoke.

Respectively: In the order given—My favorite colors are blue, green, and red, *respectively*. (Blue, and then green, and then red.)

Retroactive from/Retroactive to

Retroactive from: Do not use.

Retroactive to: This is the correct construction. Means extending back to a time in the past when certain conditions may have existed—The pay raise begins in May, but it is *retroactive to* last October.

Riffle/Rifle

Riffle: To turn hastily—She *riffled* through the book without paying much attention to it.

Rifle: A gun—I don't think the *rifle* is loaded.

Right/Rite/Write

Right: Correct; opposite of left—You are *right* that most people are *right*-handed.

Rite: A formal ceremony or a customary activity—Their *rite* of afternoon tea always included a brief talk about the day.

Write: To compose something with words or musical notes—*Write* a story about your family.

Rise: See *Raze.*

Role/Roll

Role: A part, sometimes in a play—I have the lead *role* in the movie.

Roll: To move something along smoothly, often with wheels; a type of bread—Please *roll* the car to the side of the road.

S

Say/Tell

Say: Speak; often does not have a direct object (a noun or pronoun that receives the action)—He *says* that he isn't going.

Tell: Usually involves saying something to someone. *Tell* generally has a direct object and often an indirect object as well—He *told* me a story. (He didn't *say* me a story. *Me* is the indirect object, and *story* is the direct object.)

Sea/See

Sea: Body of water—I love to vacation by the *sea.*

See: What you do with your eyes—Did you *see* that huge bird?

Seam/Seem

Seam: Place where two pieces of fabric are sewn together or where things meet—There is a tear along the *seam* of your skirt.

Seem: Appear—It *seems* to be raining harder now.

Semimonthly: See *Bimonthly.*

Sensor: See *Censor.*

Set/Sit

Set: To place something or put something; takes a direct object; you must *set* something—*Set* your books on the table.

Sit: Use without a direct object—The books *are sitting* on the table.

Sew/So/Sow

Sew: To stitch fabric—I often *sew* my own clothes.

So: The conjunction connecting words; the adverb meaning "very"—I am going on vacation, *so* I need a house sitter; a good house sitter is *so* hard to find.

Sow: To plant or scatter seeds on—We *sow* our crops in the spring.

Shall/Will

Shall: Pretty much gone from our language except in very formal writing. If you want to use *shall*, use it with first person pronouns only (*I, we*); however, in cases where you want to appear determined or for special emphasis, use *shall* for second and third person (*you, he, she, it, they*). In legal writing, *shall* has a special implication of obligation, so be careful in legal writing.

Will: Usually used for all purposes instead of *shall.*

For the colloquialism, *shall we?* (such as *Shall we dance?*), we don't use *will.* Imagine saying, *Will we dance?* It has an entirely different meaning. In this usage *Shall we dance?* means *Let's dance.*

Shined/Shone

Shined: Past tense of *shine*; often used with a direct object—I *shined* my shoes before my interview. (Direct object is *shoes*.)

Shone: Past tense of *shine*; often used without a direct object—The sun *shone* all day.

Should of: See *Could of.*

Sight: See *Cite.*

Site: See *Cite.*

Slander: See *Libel.*

So/So that

So: Used to express a result—I didn't study, *so* I failed the test.

So that: Used to express an intention—I need to study *so that* I can pass the test.

Sole/Soul

Sole: A fish; the bottom of your foot; alone—I ate fillet of *sole.*

My *sole* hurts in these shoes. She is the *sole* person living in this big house.

Soul: The spiritual essence of a person—Don't tell a *soul!* I love you with my heart and *soul.*

Some time/Sometime/Sometimes

Some time: An amount of time—I have *some time* to spend with you tomorrow afternoon.

Sometime: At some future time—You will have to come over to my house *sometime* soon.

Sometimes: Some of the time—*Sometimes* I like to eat candy all day.

Sort of: See *Kind of.*

Stationary/Stationery

Stationary: Staying in one place. You can remember this because there is an *a* in *place* and also in *stay*. Take your pick! (Yes, there is also an *e* in *place,* but it is silent.)—I just bought a *stationary* bike to ride at home.

Stationery: Paper to write on. (Does anyone use it anymore?)—My *stationery* has pretty pink flowers on it.

Statue/Stature/Statute

Statue: Three-dimensional piece of art—The *statue* of the fisherman is a popular landmark.

Stature: Height of something or achievement gained—He was very strong, although short of *stature.*

Statute: Permanent rule or enactment passed by a legislative body—The *statute* says that there be no alcohol on the premises.

Successive: See *Consecutive.*

Suppose to/Supposed to

Suppose to: Incorrect; do not use.

Supposed to: Required—You are *supposed to* tell the truth at all times.

Sure and/Sure to

Sure and: Do not use.

Sure to: Certain to do something—Make *sure to* vote on Election Day. (Not *sure and.*)

T

Tact/Tack

Tact: Knowing what to say in a difficult situation—It takes *tact* to tell a woman she doesn't look good in her favorite dress.

Tack: A short, sharply pointed nail—Put some *tacks* in the poster to hold it up.

Take: See *Bring.*

Taught/Taut

Taught: Past tense of *teach*—I *taught* school for fifteen years.

Taut: Tightly held; not slack—Hold the fabric *taut* so I can measure it accurately.

Tell: See *Say.*

Tenant/Tenet

Tenant: Someone who rents an apartment from you—My *tenant* is moving out in a month.

Tenet: Principle, doctrine, or opinion believed in by a group—One of the *tenets* of the club was to not kill animals for food or clothing.

Than/Then

Than: Used for comparison—You are taller *than* I am.

Then: An adverb referring to time—I am making dinner, and *then* I will call you back.

Note that *then* is not a conjunction, and you can't connect sentences with it unless you also use a conjunction. (*I am making dinner, then I will call you back* is not correct.)

That/Where

Do not use *where* in place of *that*. *Where* refers to a place. *That* introduces a clause.

Where are you? I know *where* you are? (Correct.)

I hear *where* the new mayor is at a fundraiser today. (Incorrect.)

I hear *that* the new mayor is at a fundraiser today. (Correct.)

Their/There/They're

Their: Possessive pronoun; belonging to them—I am *their* mother.

There: A place—Go sit over *there*. *There* are toys over *there*.

They're: A contraction meaning *they are*—*They're* with their mother over there.

Therefore: See *However.*

These/Those

These: Plural form of *this*—*These* kinds of apples grow here. (Not *these kind* of apples.)

Those: Plural form of *that* -*Those* types of foods are my favorites. (Not *those type* of foods.)

Do not use the phrases *These ones* or *Those ones.*

Threw/Through

Threw: Past tense of the verb *throw*—He *threw* the ball to his sister.

Through: Preposition—I walked *through* the doorway.

Do not use *thru* as a shortcut for *through* except in informal writing.

Throes/Throws

Throes: Turmoil; sharp attack of emotion—He was in the *throes* of a heated argument when he collapsed.

Throws: To toss something—She *throws* the ball as well as anyone on her team.

To/Too/Two

To: A preposition that tells where—I am going *to* the store.

Too: Also or overly—I am going *too*. This is *too* salty.

Two: A number—I have *two* pencils.

Note that when you use *too* at the end of a sentence, you don't need a comma before it—*I am going too.*

Toward/Towards

Use either one. They are the same. Americans generally drop the *s*; the British use the *s*.

Try and/Try to

The correct phrase is *try to*—I will *try to* finish the cleaning this morning.

U

Uninterested: See *Disinterested.*

Use to/Used to

The correct phrase is *used to*—I *used to* be an artist, but now I am a teacher.

V

Venal/Venial

Venal: Able to be purchased, for example, by a bribe—The *venal* judge was easily swayed by an offer of money.

Venial: Able to be forgiven; not seriously wrong—He had to pay only a small fine for the *venial* traffic offense of letting his registration expire.

Verses/Versus

Verses: Plural of *verse*—I know only the first two *verses* of that song.

Versus: Used in comparison—The spelling competition is the sixth-grade boys *versus* the girls.

Vicious/Viscous

Vicious: Dangerous, malicious—Lions are considered to be *vicious*.

Viscous: Of a thick and sticky consistency—The *viscous* glue got all over my clothes.

W

Waist/Waste

Waist: What gets larger when you eat cake—My *waist* measures 32 inches around.

Waste: To spend uselessly or squander—I ate the cake because I didn't want to *waste* the money I spent buying it.

Waive/Wave

Waive: To refrain from insisting on something; to forego—We *waived* some of the difficult rules, so that beginners could play the game with us.

Wave: The movement of the tides or a hand gesture in greeting—He *waved* to us before heading into the *waves* to surf.

Warrantee/Warranty

Warrantee: Person who receives a warranty—The contract applies only to the *warrantee* and his or her family.

Warranty: An agreement you get, often with a purchase, that guarantees it will work—I have a five-year *warranty* on my new washer and dryer.

Wary/Weary

Wary: On guard; watchful—I was *wary* of bears as I hiked in the woods.

Weary: Tired—I am *weary* after a long day at work.

Way/Ways

Ways: The plural of *way*. Do not use it as a singular.

How many *ways* can you solve the math problem? (Correct.)

We still have a long *ways* to go. (Incorrect—should be *way.*)

Weather/Whether

Weather: What you see when you look out the window—The *weather* is rainy today.

Whether: Implies a choice—I can't decide *whether* to go out or stay home tonight.

Well: See *Good.*

Where: See *That.*

Whet/Wet

Whet: To make eager; stimulate—These little hors d'oeuvres will *whet* your appetite for the main course.

Wet: Opposite of dry—The roads look *wet*, so I guess it rained last night.

Whether: See *If.*

Who ever/Whoever

Whoever: Some person—*Whoever* is talking loudly should stop.

Who ever: Occasionally *who* and *ever* would be two separate words; if you can put a word or phrase between them and it would all make sense, use two separate words—*Who ever* does that? (Who, I might ask, ever does that?)

Whose/Who's

Whose: Possessive—*Whose* package is this?

Who's: A contraction that means *who is*—It belongs to the man *who's* in the front row.

Will: See *Shall.*

Wont/Won't

Wont: Accustomed—He was *wont* to take a walk every afternoon.

Won't—Contraction for *will not*—I *won't* go with you this time.

Would of: See *Could of.*

Wrapped: See *Rapped.*

Write: See *Right.*

Y

Yoke/Yolk

Yoke: Something that binds together, particularly two draft animals—Take the *yoke* off those two horses.

Yolk: The yellow part of an egg—First, mix together three *yolks* to make the sauce.

Your/You're

Your: Possessive; belonging to you—Take *your* sweater when you go.

You're: Contraction meaning *you are—You're* welcome.

Part 2
Malapropisms

All of my children—Should be *all my children*. You don't need the *of* after *all*. That goes for other phrases as well: *all of the king's men* should be *all the king's men*.

Another thing coming—Although most people say it that way, the actual expression began as *another think coming*.

Meaning: To be totally wrong.

Example: If you think you're going to win, you've got *another think coming*.

Baited breath—Should be *bated breath*. *Bait* has to do with fishing.

Meaning: In a state of anticipation.

Example: I waited with *bated breath*.

Beckon call—Should be *beck and call*.

Meaning: Waiting to be of service to someone.

Example: I am at your *beck and call*.

Begs the question—Should be *raises the question*. *Begs the question* is an argument where the conclusion is already assumed in one of the premises. However, many people use the phrase *begging the question* incorrectly when they use it to mean "prompts one to ask the question."

Examples: (1) Your essay *raises the question* of why war is so prevalent in our world. (Makes the reader wonder why war is so prevalent.) (2) Since your essay seems to conclude that peace is the natural state of the world, it *begs the question* why we have so many wars. (Where is the support for your conclusion?)

Butt naked/Buck naked—Both are okay, but the original phrase is *buck naked*. *Butt naked* came into use in the 1980s.

Meaning: Completely naked.

Example: The little boy ran around the house *buck naked*.

By in large—Should be *by and large*.

Meaning: As a rule; for the most part.

Example: *By and large* this is a great place to work.

Case and point—Should be *case in point*.

Meaning: A relevant example.

Example: A *case in point* is that the number of accidents has decreased since the traffic light was added.

Chester drawers—While there may be a person named Chester Drawers, the expression is *chest of drawers*, which is exactly what it is.

Meaning: Large piece of furniture that holds your clothes.

Example: It was difficult to get the *chest of drawers* through the narrow doorway.

Cognitive dissidents—Should be *cognitive dissonance*. *Dissonance* is incongruence or things that do not match. A *dissident* is someone who disagrees.

Meaning: Beliefs and behavior that do not match each other.

Example: There seemed to be *cognitive dissidence* between what he said and how he acted toward his friends.

Deep seeded—Should be *deep seated.*

Meaning: Firmly established.

Example: My religious beliefs are *deep seated.*

Diamond dozen—Should be *dime a dozen.*

Meaning: Common.

Example: Those shirts are a *dime a dozen.*

Do diligence—Should be *due diligence.*

Meaning: To use appropriate care not to harm anyone or anything, or to investigate a person or business before signing a contract with them.

Example: Please use *due diligence* when you handle these fragile items.

Escape goat—The word is *scapegoat.* No escaping goats here!

Meaning: Someone who bears the blame for someone else.

Example: I am always the *scapegoat* when my sister does something wrong.

Expresso—That wonderful shot of caffeine is actually *espresso* with an *s,* not an *x.*

Extract revenge—Should be *exact revenge.*

Meaning: To plan revenge.

Example: He *exacted revenge* on the judge who put him in jail unfairly.

First-come, first-serve—Should be *first-come, first-served.*

Meaning: Served in the order in which you arrive.

Example: The seating for the concert is *first-come, first-served.*

Flush out—Should be *flesh out.*

Meaning: To add details to something.

Example: Please *flesh out* your essay to make it more complete.

For all intensive purposes—Should be *for all intents and purposes.*

Meaning: Virtually; practically speaking.

Example: For all *intents and purposes*, they are brothers, even though they are not related.

Hone in—Should be *home in.*

Meaning: To advance toward a target.

Example: During the practice flight, I *homed in* toward the small airport. (To *hone* is to practice a skill.)

Hunger pains—They might feel like pains, but it should be *hunger pangs.*

Meaning: To be very hungry.

Example: I haven't eaten in twelve hours, and I have *hunger pangs*!

I could care less—Should be *I couldn't care less.*

Meaning: To not care at all.

Example: *I couldn't care less* if she comes with us or not.

It's a doggy dog world—Should be *it's a dog-eat-dog world.*

Meaning: A situation where people will do anything to get ahead or get something.

Example: Professional modeling can be a very *dog-eat-dog* job.

Make due—Should be *make do.*

Meaning: To skimp by or use what is available even if it is not enough.

Example: We need to *make do* with the limited supplies that we have.

Mute point—Should be *moot point. Mute* is the inability to speak.

Meaning: A matter of no consequence.

Example: The dinner is ruined, and whether or not you are the one responsible is now a *moot point.*

Nipped in the butt—Should be *nipped in the bud.*

Meaning: To stop something before it matures.

Example: The project was *nipped in the bud* before we did much research.

On accident—Should be *by accident* although many people say *on accident.*

Meaning: Accidentally.

Example: I broke the vase, but it happened *by accident.*

On tender hooks—Should be *on tenterhooks.*

Meaning: Anxious, waiting in suspense.

Example: She waited *on tenterhooks* for her score.

One in the same—Should be *one and the same.*

Meaning: The same.

Example: These two books about dogs are *one and the same.*

Outside of the house—Should be *outside the house.* The *of* is unnecessary.

Pacifically—Should be *specifically. Pacific* is an ocean.

Meaning: With an exact use in mind.

Example: This tool is *specifically* designed for trimming leather.

Peaked my interest—Should be *piqued my interest.* This is a tricky one. *Peaked* means "to have reached the highest point." *Peeked* means "looked." *Piqued* means "aroused emotion."

Meaning: To arouse your curiosity or interest.

Example: This delicious dish *piqued my interest* in Peruvian cooking.

Piece of mind *or* **peace of mind**—Calmness brings *peace of mind.* But if you are angry, you might give someone a *piece of your mind.*

Piggybag ride—Should be *piggyback ride.*

Meaning: A ride on someone else's back or shoulders.

Example: Dad always gave me a *piggyback ride* when he came home from work.

Pigment of your imagination—Should be *figment of your imagination. Pigment* is color.

Meaning: Something that you think is real but turns out not to be.

Example: "If you think we are now friends again, it is a *figment of your imagination.*"

Prostrate cancer—Should be *prostate cancer. Prostrate* means lying down flat. The *prostate* is a male gland.

Runner-ups—Should be *runners-up.* In a hyphenated word, the more important word is made plural to make the whole word plural.

Meaning: Those who do not come in first.

Example: I was one of the *runners-up* in the dance contest.

Self-depreciating—Should be *self-deprecating.* To *depreciate* is to decrease in value. To *deprecate* is to belittle.

Meaning: Overly humble; putting oneself down.

Example: The comedian was very *self-deprecating* in his act.

Shoe-in—Should be *shoo-in.* Has nothing to do with footwear.

Meaning: Someone or something certain to win.

Example: My dog is a *shoo-in* for best poodle in the show.

Sixteenth Chapel—Should be *Sistine Chapel.* I don't think there were fifteen chapels before it.

Meaning: The chapel in the Vatican, painted by Michelangelo and other artists.

Example: One of the things Michelangelo is famous for is painting the ceiling of the *Sistine Chapel.*

Slight of hand—Should be *sleight of hand.* If you are slight of hand, maybe you have small hands. However, *sleight* means crafty or skillful.

Meaning: Skillful in movements of the hand or requiring dexterity; for example, a magician possesses this skill.

Example: I need to practice my *sleight of hand,* so people cannot figure out how I do my card tricks.

Sneak peak—Should be *sneak peek.* A *peak* is the top of a mountain. A *peek* is a quick look at something.

Meaning: Usually a look at something before it actually becomes available to view.

Example: We were able to get *a sneak peek* at the new movie before it was released to the theaters.

Spitting image/Spit and image—The original idiom was *spit and image,* from the Bible: the use of spit and mud to create Adam in his image. Now more people say *spitting image,* but the meaning is the same.

Meaning: An exact duplicate of.

Example: She is the *spitting image* of her mother.

Statue of limitations—Should be *statute of limitations.* This term has nothing to do with statues.

Meaning: The legal time limit after something happens when you are still able to begin legal proceedings.

Example: I cannot sue that doctor for malpractice because the *statute of limitations* has passed.

Step foot—Should be *set foot.*

Meaning: To enter someplace. Often used in the negative sense.

Example: Ever since the neighbor yelled at me, I have not *set foot* in his yard.

Supposively/Supposably—Should be *supposedly.*

The proof is in the putting—Should be *the proof is in the pudding.* Actually, the original idiom was *the proof of the pudding is in the eating.*

Meaning: You can't judge the success of something until you have tried it.

Example: Can you cook? I sure can. Taste this dish. *The proof is in the pudding!*

Tongue and cheek—Should be *tongue-in-cheek.*

Meaning: Something said that is facetious, not to be taken at face value.

Example: When I told you I was the best tennis player in the state, it was said *tongue in cheek.*

Note that *tongue in cheek* is hyphenated when it precedes a noun it is modifying: *tongue-in-cheek remark.*

Tow the line—Should be *toe the line.* No tow truck here.

Meaning: To do what you are expected to do.

Example: Even though I may disagree, I always *toe the line* when the boss tells me to do something.

Towards and Anyways—Should be *toward and anyway.*

Try and—Should be *try to.*

Example: Please *try to* be more careful next time.

Vicious cycle—Should be *vicious circle.*

Meaning: A negative situation that is maintained rather than being resolved.

Example: He continues to choose inappropriate jobs and then quit, continuing the *vicious circle* of unemployment.

Wet your appetite—Should be *whet your appetite.*

Meaning: To cause someone to be more interested in something.

Example: This brief introduction into classical music in intended to *whet your appetite,* so you will want to learn more about it.

Worst comes to worst/Worse comes to worse—Both are used, but it should actually be *worse comes to worst.*

Meaning: If the worst possibility should happen. Therefore, it makes more logical sense to progress from the comparative (*worse*) to the superlative (*worst*).

Example: *If worse comes to worst* and it rains for the wedding, we can always bring it indoors.

Wreck havoc—Should be *wreak havoc.*

Meaning: To cause a lot of trouble or ruin something, thus the mistake of using the word *wreck* instead of *wreak.*

Example: The constant snow will *wreak havoc* with our travel plans.

Youth in Asia—Should be *euthanasia.* They do sound similar, but *euthanasia* has nothing to do with youth in Asia!

Meaning: Ending a person's or animal's life to avoid suffering, also known as *mercy killing.*

Example: Although many people believe in *euthanasia* for terminally ill animals, many people do not.

Contact and Ordering Information

We appreciate comments and questions sent to **info@bigwords101.com.**

We also appreciate **Amazon (or Goodreads or any other) reviews** about this book and our other grammar books.

Get a free grammar book! Check out and sign up for the **Grammar Diva Blog** at
http://bigwords101.com/category/blog/

Check out the website at **www.bigwords101.com.**

All the Grammar Diva's books are available on Amazon and all other online retailers. E-books are available for Kindle and all other e-book readers.

If you would like to order bulk quantities of any of our books, contact Ingram or Baker & Taylor for print books or the iBook store for e-books.

And, finally, all our print books are available to order at any bookstore.

The Grammar Diva is available for

- **grammar talks and presentations**
- **grammar workshops**
- **copyediting and writing**

Arlene Miller

THE GRAMMAR DIVA

www.ingramcontent.com/pod-product-compliance
Lightning Source LLC
Chambersburg PA
CBHW071841020426
42331CB00007B/1814